Unspoken Love

Whispering Gaze

Nina Trivedi Soni

INDIA • SINGAPORE • MALAYSIA

Copyright © Nina Soni 2023
All Rights Reserved.

ISBN 979-8-89186-927-1

This book has been published with all efforts taken to make the material error-free after the consent of the author. However, the author and the publisher do not assume and hereby disclaim any liability to any party for any loss, damage, or disruption caused by errors or omissions, whether such errors or omissions result from negligence, accident, or any other cause.

While every effort has been made to avoid any mistake or omission, this publication is being sold on the condition and understanding that neither the author nor the publishers or printers would be liable in any manner to any person by reason of any mistake or omission in this publication or for any action taken or omitted to be taken or advice rendered or accepted on the basis of this work. For any defect in printing or binding the publishers will be liable only to replace the defective copy by another copy of this work then available.

CONTENTS

PREFACE

"Unspoken Love - Whispering Gaze" a collection of poems, is a peek into my heart. My life's tour through love, longing, pain and belonging. It explores the emotional range of my journey, touching upon my phases, from the euphoric self to a desperate one, from the ecstatic high to the lonely low.

My muse has been beyond my reach, but close to my heart.

When you are pushed to the very edge, that's when you can write.

When you fall deeply in love, that's when you can write.

Just when you think you can take it no more, that's when you can write.

When you feel so lonely that you are truly alone, that's when you can write.

Someone once said that a poet understands emotions better than others. I think, I do.

Words flow through me with the blessings of Ma Saraswati, without whom, nothing is possible.

Blessings of my Anaadi, Anant Lord Shiv, and my dear, forever close to my heart, Lord Krishna.

I'm grateful to God for giving me a gem of a person as my lover, my partner - Chetan Soni. They say, sometimes home is a person. You are that person.

Thank you God, for my beautiful kids - Reyansh and Akansh.

I want to thank my parents, Upendra Trivedi and Kumkum Trivedi for bringing me into this world and giving me the right upbringing. Thanks to my brother, Jatin Trivedi, and my family, Purvi Trivedi and Aarnavi Trivedi, for being my loved ones. I would like to thank my family - Charu Soni, Yogesh Kothari and Panna Kothari, for their love.

And most importantly, thanks to my friend, Richa Shukla, who has always loved, supported and encouraged me.

I hope you enjoy reading this book as much as I enjoyed writing it!

Yours,

Nina

1

YOUR HANDS IN MINE

I can feel your hands in my hands,
I can sense your eyes on mine.
Long after you have left,
I'm still feeling divine.

The sensation in my fingers still remain,
Although it has been a while.
The crimson on my face still stays,
And so does my smile.

Often times, I feel you are still present
Within me or in my vicinity.
Holding my heart
Tight, in your captivity.

An instinct so strong,
A realisation so profound,
Find it difficult to process,
How to deal with your sound.

Want to bring you
Right back to where you belong.
With me, close to me,
Never away from me, a relation so strong.

2

INTENSE GAZE

I check across the crowded room,
I see you staring at me.
Leaning against the wall,
No obstruction in view, just you and me.

The music starts to play,
When our eyes begin to sing,
We understand the lyrics,
And the melody starts to ring.

Still unaware of the world around,
We keep conversing with our gaze,
The orbs know the language we speak,
Although the body seems to be in a daze.

Replying to every question,
Countering your every censure,
I have a reason for not seeing you for days,
I understand your displeasure.

No more will I stay far from your sight,
I want to say this aloud.
But the world around magically appeared
And I keep my voice under the shroud.

We are highly confidential,
And that's what makes it a thrill.
I wouldn't want it any other way,
Even if hiding is a task uphill.

The pretensions will all dissipate one day,
The truth would surely be out,
I'm not worried or scared.
Because for us, I don't have any doubt.

3

DEEP IN LOVE

I've not returned
From where I left myself,
I'm still there, if you see,
Trying to free myself from your clutches.

The circle of your arms around me
Has engulfed my heart and soul.
Your imaginary touch
Has swallowed me whole.

There is no escape,
Gladly, I don't want any.
No respite from your thoughts
However uncanny.

It's the way you look at me.
That's the culprit.
It's that half smile,
That I find unable to resist.

You are the missing piece
Of my life's jigsaw.
The traces of my lost innocence,
The very last straw.

It's like I'm back to my
Teenage crush days,
When I could smile when alone,
When I would be a blushing mess.

When I could spend hours
Just being in love,
Not responding to anyone's call,
Not a push nor a shove.

I relive every fraction
Of my moment in your company.
Hoping I can recreate them
By just revisiting my memory.

I'm, at this very moment,
Experiencing life's most beautiful feeling.
No, don't get close;
I need just you and me, vibing.

I hold my heart
While you hold my hand.
You just get close
And my heart can't understand

How hard to beat or how fast.
It's now at your command.
I've lost all power over it,
It's just as you demand.

"Bliss" is what I can call it,
No other word to say.
I don't want to go back again
From where I went astray.

If astray or delinquent
Is what you call it.
Sinner if I am,
Who is the one to judge it?

A moment more,
Before it disappears
It feels like minutes,
But it has been hours....

Transient like the dew drops in the morning
Or like the flick of the chin,
Fleeting like a jiffy,
Ephemeral like a goblin.

It is clairvoyance,
I see you and I together,
Being with each other,
Smiling in a trance.

A happy augury is what it is,
I saw you in my dream.
Close to me, walking with me,
As content as we may seem.

4

SWEET INTOXICATION

The words in your eyes
And the look on your lips,
I understand it all, the sweet intoxication of your scent,
I never fail to recall.

The memory of the moments
Spent with you, can't be erased.
Sends me back to those times,
Leaves me completely dazed.

Your words are music
To my ever eager ears.
Your song and rhythm,
I can be attuned to for years.

When you talk,
I stop listening and at you, I just gaze,
When you are silent, I hear
Your heartbeats and I stay unfazed.

I feel your presence in the air
When you pass by me.
Touching me soft,
Letting me free.

Engulfed by you,
I feel at liberty.
No restraint, no regret,
Just beautiful synergy.

Confines of my mind
Finally opened!
Nothing to hold back,
Shackles broken.

My heart feels like a free bird,
Reaching for the skies.
Don't want to be beneath the stars,
Beyond that it flies.

5

MELTING A GLACIER WITH A GLANCE

Melting a glacier
With a glance,
Is what I call you now,
While I'm in a trance.

That hand on my cheek
Still there, not left,
The sensation sending shivers,
I was long bereft.

Dry as a desert,
My life was of love,
Yearning and longing
For fulfilment, I strove.

Your song's lilting music
Is playing on my fingers.
It's been long since I heard it,
But the tune still lingers.

Being stuck in that moment
Is what I am right now.
No matter how much I try
Don't know how.

The color of the moon,
The hue of the sun,
Can't paint my heart different
From the one that you burn.

The wind that blows on my face,
Can't erase the memory of those days.
When I smiled when there was nothing to smile about
When I just passed out in a daze.

Have heard that there can always be first love
But never a last,
No matter how hard you try,
Nothing stays steadfast.

Because love never ceases
But love ever bends.
It changes forms and means,
It also changes ends.

Unfulfilled was I left,
Without the warmth of your arms.
Brimming eyes with tears,
Sweaty but very cold palms.

The chapters of my life are
Full of pages about you.
When you read it someday,
You will know what I'm due.

6

ACROSS THE ROOM

I glanced across the room,
Waiting for some miracle to happen.
I see you looking at me,
And I stood there completely frozen.

Laying eyes on you after a long time,
Still missing a heartbeat sure.
I knew you would be there
With your charming self and heart so pure.

You make your way towards me,
And my pulse goes completely crazy.
You smile and greet me,
Does your heart beat as fast? Maybe.

I steady my nerves but hold my breath,
We converse with ease.
Your quick remarks are met with
My answers with sass.

We laugh at each other's jokes,
Our smiles reach our eyes.
Yours reaches my heart too,
No question of any lies.

I blush incessantly,
I can't help it.
Anyone who sees us, will know,
I can't hide it a bit.

I can hear you whisper in my ears,
My heart can hear your silence too,
My eyes can read what you wish to say,
My soul connects to these feelings anew.

I feel, I already know your secrets
And you know mine.
A different line of communication runs through us,
Not a word, just a sign…

I hope that it's the beginning of something lovely,
A love story maybe, why not?
A book full of hues and shades,
Just a passing thought.

7

YOUR EYES STOLE MY POETRY

Laughing without any reason,
Blushing all the way to my eyes,
Smiling at everyone I see,
Why have I become like this?

I had prepared words to say to you,
Several sonnets, beautiful lyrics too,
A ballad or epic somehow,
A composition in verses true.

But your eyes stole all my poetry,
I couldn't remember even a word of the memoirs,
No matter how hard I tried to frame it,
My mind was blocked by your twin stars.

They stared at me like there was no tomorrow,
I shied with my eyes downcast.
My face, a crimson deep,
My heart, a crazy fast.

His voice, so deep and profound,
Called me, by my name aloud.
I brought myself back to this world,
Tapping my head, holding my ground.

He spoke to me on a calm note.
What? I don't know.
I wasn't listening, just staring
At the sparkles, nodding with the flow.

He heard my heart beating for him,
He smiled a knowing one,
He stopped talking and stood gawking,
Syncing it with mine, emotions undone.

Words don't stand a chance,
When it comes to us.
We might as well give up talking
And let eyes have all the fun.

Let our hearts sort out its issues,
Let the souls collide,
Let the vibes get along,
We, with our words, just move aside.

8

STILL ART, WITHOUT YOU

I won't tell him.
I think, he knows.
He won't say anything either
Or do anything that shows.

Your heart beats for mine
My eyes blink for yours.
My breath, it always hitches
Whenever you get close.

When you sing the song,
I know it's about me.
I feel serenaded by you,
I imagine you have taken the knee.

All the words penned by me,
Are actually conversations with you.
Wish I could read it aloud one day
And tell you my feelings true.

Often, I do wonder,
Had we not met ever?
Were there already emotions in me?
Words coming out for an endeavour?

Had you not stirred feelings inside?
Had you not upset the Apple cart?
If you hadn't created ripples within,
Had you not stolen my heart?

My world would have remained
An Art, so still,
Colours and shades would be there,
But no movement, no thrill.

Have dreamt about us that one day,
Unafraid, we will be of everyone.
Aloud, we will confess to ourselves,
Shouting loudly, till the horizon.

9

EYES TRUER THAN WORDS

Words often lie,
But eyes, they are true.
They convey our feelings,
They uncover the soul through.

That's why I prefer
To just stare at you.
Talk through our eyes,
Don't need a word or two.

The misty, the radiant, the golden look.
The fixated, the dazzling, the lustrous look.
The tender, the meaningful, the understanding look.
But nothing beats the smitten look…

I'm still not over your gazes,
The glances that we steal at each other,
The bright and lit-up hue of the face,
Oh, the thrill that we get from each other!

Every time you pass me by,
The sparkling look that I see.
When you leave my sight,
The hopeful look is what I plea.

Words don't hold any water,
To the beautiful language that we speak.
Eyes, heart, soul know it all,
Now, nothing else I would seek.

The outcome of this is unknown.
Because no answer to any question is sought.
It's just the feeling here and now,
Just the rush of love thought.

Finally, a moment of truth dawns
On each of us, as we dare,
We can't be with each other,
No matter how much we care.

Life's journey is a string of moments,
Tied together with the time present.
No room for contrition or regrets,
No chance for guilt or resent.

Let's take a chance with life,
Let's do a gamble,
Let's wager everything we've earned,
Giving us no room to scramble.

I'm bold enough, I know,
About you, I'm still unsure.
Eyes, looks, heartbeat is fine,
But to you, my step may seem immature.

Unanswered, my prayers will always be,
Unreciprocated, my love.
Fruitless, will be the result of my efforts,
Pining always, my heart's treasure trove.

10

ARE WE SINNERS?

I'm lost in a sea of emotions
When I look in your eyes,
Like all my feelings are writ large
On my face, snapping all other ties.

It's a sight to behold,
When the world has come to a standstill,
We stare at each other
Intently, till we have our fill.

My love for you
Unconditional and pure,
Can be seen in every glance
Radiating from me, eyes still unsure.

Will there ever be a day,
In this realm, in this lifetime,
When we can be comfortable to talk face to face
When we let us feel sublime?

Will we always be sinners?
Do we have to stay forever apart?
Seeking eyes, aching souls,
Hurting emotions, wounded heart?

11

HEART'S EMPTY SPACE

It was in the still of the night,
I heard some voices.
I think it was from inside of me.
Some of them shouts, some whispers
From heart's empty spaces.

Was it a cry for help?
Or was it an appeal to be heard?
Can ignore it no more,
Can't silent the bard.

The heart, it wants to sing,
The eyes that want to behold,
The lips that want to smile,
The hand that wants to hold.

No holds, no bars,
No walls, no locks.
Not anyone with lofty ideals,
No waves stopped by the rocks.

Unbridled, unstoppable,
Unreined but understood,
Unbreakable and uncontrolled
Someone truly unprude…

The colors that I breathe,
Are of the seven that you see.
Yet, it's not the hue you know,
Not easy for me to show.

There can only be
You for me and me for you.
Well, doesn't work anymore.
I'm no longer the same person, as before.

Duality of existence,
Body and soul,
Or is it searching for oneness
Of the universe as a whole?

Try to define something
And you confine it.
Try to feel it
You liberate it.....

12

IN YOUR ARMS

In your arms, I sit.
Without a worry at all.
Beaming from ear to ear,
Sensing the world stall.

Is it comfortable or exciting?
Stimulating or bliss?
Can't figure out,
Real emotional mess.

Never ready to give up,
Not willing to let go.
Can't leave your hand,
Can't stop the flow.

You never know how frozen you are
Until someone starts to melt your ice.
Nor do you know how lost you are,
Until someone finds you and takes you to new heights.

The solace that I find in you,
Can be found nowhere else.
Sitting with you, hand in hand,
Enjoying the happiness that dwells.

13

YOU ARE MY SECRET

You can be my little secret,
You can be my maybe,
You can be my eternal hope,
My covert kept safely.

No secret rendezvous,
No clandestine meetings,
Just stealing glances at each other,
Very meaningful greetings.

Silence on our lips,
Silent our eyes too.
Conversing in each other's thoughts
Talking with our heartbeats true.

When we meet, we feign indifference,
When we meet, we just pretend
To be unaffected by each other.
Well, you are just a friend.

There will come a time, I hope,
When we let down our guard,
When we speak out our heart,
When the world, we just disregard.

Pretensions can't be forever,
Conscience is what is true,
No matter how much we act,
No regrets, yes, nothing to rue.

There is a possibility
That our emotions betray us,
Our love may show itself by a blush,
Or a sparkle in our eye, so sus..

14

INFINITE LOVE

What is love if not infinity times forever?
Is there anything like an infinite or ever-flowing river?

All merges into something,
Infinite into the defined
And river into the sea.

Then it's never the same
Ever again.
It's a sum
That loses more than it gain.

We fill up the empty spaces
Within us, with each other.
Like a jigsaw puzzle or
Like sugar to water.

Bit by bit I melt in you
And embrace you in our ecstasy.

It's more spiritual
Than real.
Not seen by us,
Just felt - surreal?

Yearning is fulfilling
Not fulfillment.
Bliss is not what I seek
What I want is longing....

Pining for what I seek,
Driving me to the edge.
Will not say precipice,
Cause I mean bondage.

Don't want the desire to be fulfilled.
Because fulfilled is the end.
There may be nothing beyond equilibrium,
Staying still is not what I intend.

15

FACE TO FACE

Eyes overwhelmed,
Heart beats fast,
Lips quivering,
Will I last?

Surviving the onslaught
Of unrequited love,
Unfulfilled desires,
Unending emotional flow.

When suddenly, I come face-to-face
With someone unknown,
Love, wishes come true,
And satisfactory winds blown.

It's this that I don't want,
I'm happy in my little space
Of yearning, craving for love
And for better days.

♥♥♥

16

SHOW OF LOVE

Love has a mysterious way
To make your day
Bright and beautiful,
From sad and resentful.

Just a glimpse of you
Is all I seek.
A pat on the head,
A touch on the cheek.

A show of love
At its peak
Is a hug so tight,
Too brave for the meek.

A lingering gaze
For not more than a couple of seconds,
Is what I hoped for
As far as I reckon.

Do sunsets and serenity go together?
For me, it's when I'm with you.
It sets me free,
It's what makes us true.

The sound that you don't make,
I can hear loud and clear.
Everything about you,
I hold so close and dear.

Just breathe easy, my love,
It's not right to stress.
You take my breath away
Without a kiss or caress.

A love so pristine,
A feeling so pure,
No demands,
No expectations to endure…

17

I CAN'T BE YOUR STORY

I can't be your story,
Just your desire.
Can be just some ice,
Can't be your fire.

I wish to be your moment
Full of deep love.
Can't be a lifetime,
Just a small lip curve.

A glimpse of you
For a few seconds
Is all I want,
As far as I reckon.

No touch needed,
A glance is enough
To race my heart
Through smooth and rough.

A smile towards me
And an unspoken word
Communicated by eyes
As fast as a fleeting bird.

My heart knows when
Your heart beats
In sync with mine.
A connect so divine.

A gaze from you
Directed at me,
Helps in moving me
Closer to ecstasy.

♥ ♥ ♥

18

I'M THE HEART

When my eyes can no longer hide
The love that I have for you,
They will overflow
With feelings that are so pure and true.

You heal my heart
That you haven't broken.
You occupy a space in me
That has never been taken.

You are that remaining part of me
That fits perfectly like a mole.
You complete me, my dear,
You make me whole.

My life has come a full circle
When I'm not just fulfilling a part.
I'm glad, I'm not just a booster,
I'm a rocket, I'm the heart.

♥ ♥ ♥

19

WHEN YOU ARE CLOSE TO ME

My heart, it missed a beat,
My eyes, they didn't blink.
I just filled myself with you,
Letting the feeling sink.

Fidgety fingers,
Unsteady feet,
Brimming eyes,
Unsettled heartbeat.

When you are close to me,
I keep falling for you.
For a tiny million things,
You don't know that you do.

I'm left speechless
When you look in my eye.
Can't balance my mind,
No matter how hard I try.

My longing for you
Seeks a belonging now.
Can wait no more,
Want you here and now.

I think, waiting is killing,
Yearning is so cruel.
The feeling can tear you apart
It's like getting your gruel.

Trust me to deal with the pain,
On me, you can lay your head.
The journey is very long,
But with you beside me, I'm not afraid.

Embarking on this path,
With roses and thorns,
Have to deal with snickers,
Giggles and scorns.

Do I look like someone
Who would care what others think?
No matter how much anyone pushes,
Can't bring me to the brink.

It's my inner self that I'm afraid of,
It's the lofty ideal I stand for.
My conscience is watching me,
I'm shaken to the core.

20

SILENCE BETWEEN US

You know some words will never be said,
Some feelings never expressed.
Our eyes will always be longing,
Our emotions will stay suppressed.

Each lip bite has a story to tell,
Some honest tale not disclosed.
Every time I avoid your gaze,
It's like an open chapter closed.

Silence between us
Is deafeningly loud.
Heart jumping to reveal,
Lips wanting to say it aloud.

Hesitating feet, close to you,
Hands eager to hold,
Eyes searching for you,
Waiting to behold.

All of me stay unfulfilled.
Hands, eyes and heart.
Have somehow told myself
That we are still not apart.

I don't want to be an audience
Of my own life unfolding,
I'm tired of waiting for chances that fate would give,
To get a look at you - my eyes beholding.

We don't belong to each other, I know,
But a fleeting second of togetherness is all I seek.
Trying to be as strong as I can be,
Before I really turn weak.

♥ ♥ ♥

21

I'M REALLY HAPPY

Rest easy, my dear,
It's a long night.
A night of peace and tranquil,
Where the moon and stars are bright.

Will not call upon the heavens
To deal with my pain today.
I'm really happy
As on my soft bed, I lay.

A glimpse of you is enough
To get me through the rough.
Your thoughts, I behold later,
What I feel, doesn't matter.

I close my eyes and see you again,
It's you! And I'm smiling through my pain.
Can we heal each other?
By staying away from each other?

Are you the cause or are you the cure?
How long do I have to endure?
Oscillating between pain and healing,
This indecision is killing.

One day, the inner struggle will end.
The world will understand and bend.
We shall be free from shackles,
No more war of love and no more internal battles.

22

LETTING GO

I feel sad but I got to let it go
And open a new chapter
Of my life and love
With a new character.

I want to set you free
From the web of my love,
If ever I were to believe,
Something we were above.

If something were to remain unfinished,
Let it be a beautiful art!
Incomplete, but not for the world,
Just in your and mine's heart.

Releasing myself from your encompassing thoughts,
Your vibes, your scent,
Fearing the vacuum that I'm going to be in,
Without you being present.

So it's going to be a new day,
With no you, and no me with you.
There can be a me without you,
But it's never going to be the same.

Birds will keep chirping,
But the ears, they just fold.
The flowers blossom,
But I'm not there to behold.

I heard that in the larger scheme of things,
One flower less to blossom
Will hurt Mother Nature
Right in her bosom.

Then why my tears don't affect
The balance of nature?
Why my unfulfilled love
Is it not a bother?

I want to fight this something above
Which all call destiny.
Why my feelings are questioned,
Always under scrutiny?

In another realm, in another world,
If there is any,
I will find you and choose you in a hundred lifetimes,
In all versions of reality.

23

STEADY MY HEART

Have seen you a million times
In person and in my dreams.
What is it that makes me nervous?
Like the first time, it seems.

I try to steady my heart,
When I'm in your vicinity.
There's something about you
That leads me to infinity.

Harmonizing is healing,
They say.
Syncing is appealing.
But I'm not doing it, no way.

Why do I ignore you?
Why do I avoid you?
Not because I don't like you
But I'm afraid of falling for you.

The blush that you bring to my face
Is visible to all,
The racing heartbeats, the rise in heat,
Easy for my heart to fall.

Nothing beats the pink
That you bring on my cheek,
Purest of emotions,
Too hard to take for the weak.

24

ARE WE DESTINED TO BE TOGETHER?

The love that's not written in our stars,
I see it in our eyes.
No matter how much we hide,
No matter how much we disguise.

Do you believe in Destiny? I do.
Had you been in mine,
We would be together
With the help of the Divine.

I accept what my life has to offer,
You with me or me alone.
Life goes on, without you too,
I will go on, on my own.

I don't know what end we look at
Or how far we can foresee.
Life's momentary,
We have to set it free.

It's about the present moment really,
There is no always and forever.
I don't believe in "till eternity"
It's only now or never.

If today you can't be mine
And I'm held back by the chains on my feet,
Can't think of how tomorrow can bring us together,
Loud and open, or discreet.

Let's call it providence,
That we got to be with each other.
You lit up my heart with hope
As a friend, not a lover.

There are doors that we can't walk through,
There are windows we can't look from.
Walls that only divide
And roofs that just hide.

Our destiny stops us
From finding love in each other.
Even if we do,
We would not take it further.

Although I seem very brave now,
I fear the vacuum that you will leave inside me.
I'm afraid that I will stop feeling alive,
I will lose all emotions inside me.

Is it that I want to disappear?
Or that I want my pain to?
Let's make a deal with Fate,
To make all this a falsehood, not true.

This is too heavy a burden to carry alone,
I'm left feeling like a soldier lone,
Fighting the emotions inside me,
Battling the conflicts within.

25

MY HEART HAS GROWN WINGS!!

My heart seems to have grown wings,
The smile has not left my eyes.
A flight mode is what I'm in now,
My soul, it just flies.

Fleeting, upbeat emotions,
Reappeared in my world.
I'm on cloud nine again,
My prayers finally answered.

Hopes awakened,
Expectations rise,
Sun's still on the horizon,
I just got to realise.

Is the muse back?
And with a vengeance too?
Can't hold back anymore,
I have to be with you.

Can the walls be broken?
Can the river be crossed?
Can the earth be shaken?
Can the ideal be lost?

It's the barriers that I have to break,
It's the mental block that has to melt,
For a river to break free,
A thousand tremors were felt.

26

MY LIFE, A RIVER COURSE!

When a river flows,
She doesn't care for the mountains she crosses
Or the valleys
She leaves behind.
She still carries a part of each of them with her.

But when the river makes up her mind to merge herself with the sea,
She sheds all that she holds along her way
And enters the sea with force.

I carried all with me,
My lover in my heart,
My babies in my womb,
Responsibilities on my head.

When I merge with my Soulmate,
I'm going to shed all these.
A state of ultimate bliss!

No love, no responsibility,
Just a rapid flow into the vast ocean of self-consciousness.
Into the state of equilibrium
State of oneness with my Only One!

27

NO WORDS

Words often are no help
When I want to explain my feeling,
It will degrade the meaning.

What I need is a touch,
Which can be a medium
For the flower to bloom.

Words can never capture,
How often does my heart beat.
Only we can understand
When our eyes meet.

My eyes speak in a language
No sentences can explain.
They tell stories of my dreams,
That would otherwise just remain.

My world sparkled with joy,
When I caught a glimpse of him.
My look softened with tenderness,
When my captive gaze held him.

Eyes can say everything,
Only if you listen to it with your heart
No stars, no destiny,
Can now keep us apart.

28

NEGATIVITY

Negativity draining my energy,
Making me hollow.
How do I get rid of it?
How to deal with the blow?

Tried indifference,
Confronted too.
But to no avail.
It still sucks me through.

Bad Vibes killing my positives,
Spoiling my zone.
Would want to go away
Far from all this, all alone.

Ruining my life game,
Depleting my living years,
Nothing I want more now,
Than be away from tears.

Like my solitude better,
Like to be in my cocoon shell,
Just my loved ones with me,
Only the ones with whom I gel…

29

HIS GAZE

His gaze held me tight,
His aura ensnared me,
His words held my breath,
His presence enthralled me.

I was mesmerized
By the sound of his voice,
The rest of the world just muted,
No din, no noise.

His melody lilted in my heart
Long after it was over.
The tune played again and again,
Like the continuous fragrance of a flower.

The memory of his smile,
The eagerness in his behavior,
Set my heart apace,
Left me with a sweet flavour.

Will our world ever be filled with words?
Or will the silence always speak?
Have waited too long for either of us
To gather courage and squeak.

Will a conversation break the illusion
That we nurse for each other?
Will words kill our fantasy
That we daydream with each other?

Is it advisable to live in an oasis
And enjoy the mirage once in a while?
Or is it okay to climb out of imagination
And leave the emotions with a smile....

30

WHEN YOU APPEARED BEFORE ME

Life came to a standstill,
The moment you came into my view.
It wasn't for the first time,
It wasn't anything new.

I asked my heart to
Stop speeding up,
Directed my pulse to
Stop freeing up.

Calm down, my dear,
But frayed nerves were wrecking,
Could hold myself in no more,
I just stayed gawking.

The sweetest shot in my world,
Is nothing short of your name.
The sound that it makes, is soothing,
I say it again and again.

All I want, is my dream
To be manifested into reality,
To have it happen to us,
Fulfilling a prophecy.

31

EQUILIBRIUM OR EXTREMES?

If it doesn't make you crazy,
It's not true love.
If you can still function with your head,
It would just be a fraction thereof.

It's not enough effort,
If you are not pushing to the edge.
It's not near enough,
If it's working on the fringe.

A whisper in the ear,
Would often suffice.
Needn't be a shout
Or a loud cry.

It's not music,
If it doesn't touch the cord within,
If it doesn't give you jitters or tears,
Or stirs up something within.

Equilibrium is nothing,
It's the extremes that are real.
Equilibrium is just Utopia,
Never to be achieved, just surreal.

Sleepless nights and butterflies,
Signify the uncalm nerves.
It's the shivers that are true,
Not the opinion she reserves.

The blush narrates a true story,
Of a fast beating heart.
It's the eyes that portray
An honest tale, right from the start.

Words can never explain,
The sincere state of proclivity.
It's the look that conveys
How love holds one in captivity.

It's never the mediocre that is remembered,
It always takes an extra mile.
To reach the echelons of success,
Pass the fire test by trial.

32

I'M HAPPY THAT YOU EXIST

I'm happy that you exist,
I'm glad that you are,
You are the reason I resist,
Temptations to run afar.

The melody of your song,
Wipes off the malady of my heart.
I want to hear it again and again,
Never want us to be apart.

My home has always been
Your arms around me,
No matter where we are,
It just sets me free.

Trapped in your gaze,
Ensnared in your sight,
Why do I feel completely liberated?
Why do I feel it's right?

I feel lonely in a crowd,
When you are not around.
In your presence, I feel safe, not lost,
I feel, I'm found.

Our world is surely meant to be.
We may get far away from each other.
Fate will bring us back in unison,
Luck will get us together.

33

ONE-SIDED LOVE

Can I still love you
When you can't love me back?
One-sided love is often enough
When it's not written in our zodiac.

We drift far away from each other,
Despite our hearts beating as one.
We stay longing for each other,
As if it's strictly forbidden.

Never had I fathomed,
The distance between us would be so large,
I kept hoping against hope,
I thought, I was the one in charge.

Kept my fingers crossed,
For every knock on my door,
I would wish and hope it would be you,
I kept praying more and more!

I stare into emptiness amidst a crowd,
It's no one, if it's not you.
My heart feels heavy and at unease,
Living on the edge, waiting for you.

34

HAVE I EVER?

Have I ever brought a smile to your face?
Have you ever been happy because of me?
Has my thought ever given you thrills?
Have you ever with your stares kissed me?

Have you ever lost your sleep because of me?
Or slept well because I existed?
Have you ever had unspoken words in your heart,
Which you wanted to say, but resisted?

Have my thoughts ever brought tears to your eyes?
Has there ever been a moment,
You wanted me to be with you,
But thought it better to be prudent?

Has my presence ever skipped your heartbeat?
Like mine does every time.
Has it suffered somersault like mine does?
Just crazy, it flips every time.

Has the question 'What if'
Ever occurred to you?
Have you ever considered an alternative?
If I had been with you?

Maybe in another version of reality,
We resonate with each other.
That version is a version of our desires,
Our dreams coming of age, finally we are together!

35

I DON'T SAY YOUR NAME

I don't ever say your name
Nor do I ever mention you,
You pushed me towards my goal,
I'm ever so grateful.

A piece of you is always there
In every word I write,
In every word I speak,
In every tear on my cheek.

I put you deep inside me,
Not to be found by even me.
I deserve to be happy though,
Even if, without you, I just can't be.

Slept many nights in the hope
To see you in my dreams,
Spent many sleepless nights too,
Pushing me to the extremes.

Will there ever be a time,
When this nameless emotion we recognize?
When we would feel free to express,
Without the need to apologise.

Only then, remorseless will be our love,
Impenitent, our living,
You and I, in this world,
Happy and together, God willing.

36

A WHISPER

A Whisper is all I need,
To set your imagination on fire.
A whisper is enough to
Make you smug, but invoke everyone's ire.

Just a low voice,
If I want to get my point across.
Just the keyword with a smile,
For your heart to flip a toss.

Soft murmurs are adequate,
If it's just to soothe your fluttering nerves,
Just a hint or sigh a little,
For the eye that only flirts.

Who needs to say so many words?
Unnecessary would be a lengthy verse.
Just a blink or better still a wink,
To make you a little nervous.

A smile on my face is enough
To light up your world within.
Why do we speak at all?
When the visage can take you for a spin.

When the aura is conducive,
When the vibes are right,
Holding hands is the best communication,
For the forever fire to ignite.

37

CAN FEELINGS FADE AWAY?

Can feelings fade away?
Can thoughts gather dust?
Can it be possible that one day,
I would forget you, if I must.

The sleepless nights that I spent,
Wondering whether you were awake,
Suddenly, would turn into enduring indifference,
Gone would be my heartache.

That longing in my eyes,
No longer shows.
The sparkle in those twins long gone,
They have learned to compose.

The heartbeat is upbeat no more,
They don't skip like before,
They don't race too,
No fluttering or pounding anymore.

There is dullness in my eyes,
No glitter in them now.
Is it the heartbreak that hurts
Or is it his indifference,
That has bothered me somehow?

The skip in the step
In anticipation of meeting him,
Has been replaced by a sense of resignation.
Now, the condition looks grim.

World full of hope
Has been replaced with despair.
Your disinterest had brought in
Doubt and fear, beyond repair.

Survive, I will, surely though,
Despite all these adversities.
It's not what you get but what you make of it,
That will sail you through the complexities.

The void that filled my heart,
Can be replaced by compassion.
If not your love, then
Let it be my obsession.

The emptiness within,
Is no longer so.
Filled to the brim with your songs,
I'm singing with the flow.

The tears don't fill up in my eyes,
Like it used to earlier,
They have dried up,
Still haven't found anyone worthier.

The glow in my eyes can return, for sure,
I can't let you have all the powers.
Yes, no one can replace you,
But it's destiny that always overpowers.

38

YOU WERE UNDECIDED

I kept loving him forever,
He was still skeptical,
He kept it unconfirmed,
And here, I was waiting for a miracle.

I was quite certain that we were meant to be,
He was still equivocal about us,
I never got any clarity.
Still, I accepted him without a fuss.

He would not see me eye to eye,
And here, I was longing to gaze,
He would avoid being open about us
And I was expected to stay unfazed?

Love, I realised much later
Was becoming a lover,
Not finding one.
It's oneself that we discover.

Why pursue you then?
Why not focus on me instead?
Your uncertainty surely bothered me
That madness I need to shed.

If stars align and you become determined,
I would want us to gravitate hand in hand.
Not sitting on the fence, not vague,
Confident and positive, footprints on the sand.......

39

GAME OF FATE

When fate is in the mood to play,
A game that is so not fair,
I see you from afar but can't reach you,
And you are not even aware.

When luck decides that
You and I should breathe the same air,
But not knowing that the distance is not much,
I'm looking for you everywhere.

When fortune would smile on us
And we would smile at each other too,
We might be able to steal a glance,
Without anyone having a clue.

If stars stay true to my prayers,
Then we would meet again soon,
In this one or another life,
I would be over the moon.

If Providence decides one day,
That you will be mine and I, yours.
Nothing else will stand in our way,
We will glide together, away to farther shores.

40

YOU MADE MY LIFE BEAUTIFUL

You came into my life
And I became more beautiful.
Yes, you pushed all my negatives away
And made my life bountiful.

I wanted to be the person,
You would love and cherish forever,
I upped my game just for you,
I wanted to be yours forever.

My world blossomed into a flower,
Just because you were in it.
The colors and the fragrance burst into my life
Because of the light you lit.

I didn't know God sent you
For a specific purpose.
That I should learn to live with longing,
With tears and with remorse.

Autumn follows the summer,
And winter, the autumn.
How did I not know that after blooms, come the fall?
How could I have forgotten?

It's beautiful, without you too,
I've come to live with the cold.
Your coldness and the weather too,
All my miseries stay untold.

I cry no more that I've lost but
Rejoice, that I've loved at least once.
A complete cycle of love and loneliness,
Now, I take it as it comes.

41

IN LOVE?

How can your touch decide
Whether I live or die?
How can your smile
Send shivers through my spine?

Why do your eyes search
If I'm around or away?
Why do your vibes
Want to sync with mine?

What is it that I want to hear?
For more than the past one year.

Your words play the music
That I wanted to compose.
With you around,
My heart has no repose.

It beats like crazy, in rhythm though.
As if it's the same music that I heard before….

What is it about you or about me?
Or should I say, what is it about us
That starts the light?
Need no fire for sparks to ignite.

It's always special
When we are together.
Never a dull moment,
Just thoughts to gather.

Sometimes words,
Sometimes silence,
Unspoken volumes
In just a glance.

Will I ever return?
To where I was before
Will I be able to find
That person of yore?

A soul transformed,
A life refined.
Another world,
Things undefined.

Nothing to express,
No words to say,
A connect so lovely,
(Maybe another day).

Bliss, euphoria, ecstasy!
Is what I'm feeling right now.
Am I in love again?
Is it possible? How?

Letting loose
My heart and feet,
You can run huge strides
And my heart, you can beat!

Should I call it freedom at last?
From a mundane existence.
Is that it?
No resistance?

At a stage in life, where
It's easy to say "Who cares?"
I wish it were true for all,
Only the one who dares.

This deliverance, I will never let go

This emancipation, is something that I got to behold.

Yes, it's Freedom at last

From the shackles of time,

When the world stands still

And you would be mine.

42

JOURNEY INWARDS

Journey towards myself,
Is what I call this phase I'm in.
Being able to love myself completely and unconditionally
And what I aim to be within.

I want to be near myself,
Be able to hear myself.
My heartbeats and the butterflies,
See clear myself....

When I close my eyes, I feel as if I'm going inwards,
Looking in for results and rewards.
Deep inside of me,
Making some inroads.

Hey, me? Do you know me?
I'm you and you are me.
Not two but one.
But then who talks and who hears?

Soul to the body

Or body to the soul?

Inseparable, till together,

For a long time, I hope....

Reach Out to the Author:

: NINA TRIVEDI SONI

: NTCS0212

www.ingramcontent.com/pod-product-compliance
Lightning Source LLC
LaVergne TN
LVHW091117150826
845673LV00002B/867